The Good Behavior Book

A Behavior Management Program for Families

By Michael Martin
Edited by Stephen Harris Ph.D

Copyright © 1989, and 2024 by *Michael Martin*
All rights reserved.
No portion of this book may be reproduced in any form without written permission from the publisher or author, except as permitted by U.S. copyright law.
This publication is designed to provide accurate and authoritative information in regard to the subject matter covered. It is sold with the understanding that neither the author nor the publisher is engaged
in rendering legal, medical, psychological or other professional services. While the publisher and author have used their best efforts in preparing this book, they make no representations or warranties with respect to the accuracy or completeness of the contents of this book and specifically disclaim any implied warranties of merchantability
or fitness for a particular purpose. No warranty may be created or extended by sales representatives or written sales materials. The advice and strategies contained herein may not be suitable for your situation. You should consult with a professional when appropriate. Neither the publisher nor the author shall be liable for any loss of profit or any other commercial damages, including but not limited to special, incidental, consequential, personal, or other damages.
Book Cover by Rebeka Cardenas
Illustrations by Andrew Knight and Rebeka Cardenas
Editing by Brett Weiss
YourLegacyYourStory.com

Third edition 2023

"This book is dedicated to families who want to establish and reinforce everyday good behaviors and a more harmonious household."
–Michael Martin

Table of Contents

Preface..6
The Behavior Board...8
CHAPTER I..**10**
    Using the Behavior Board..10
    Overview..10
    Good vs. Bad Behaviors..10
    Observation...11
    Pinpointing (labeling)..11
    Tracking..14
    Starting the Observation...15
    Pinpointing and Tracking Period...15
    Goal Setting..19
    Rewards and Reinforcers..23
    Establishing Priorities...25
    Starting the Game...26
    Giving Stars (or Points)...35
    Changing Behaviors and Rewards..36
    Frequently Asked Questions About the Behavior Board.......38
    Time Is On Your Side..42
CHAPTER II...**43**
    Counting...43
CHAPTER III..**53**
    Time Out..53
    What Exactly Is Time Out?...54
    When to Use Time Out...54
    How to Use Time Out...55
    Time Out Away from Home..61
    In the Car..61
    In a Restaurant...62
    In Retail Stores...63
    In Grocery Stores..63
CHAPTER IV..**64**
    Other Uses of Time..65

Preface

Good behavior is one of the most important things we learn in our youth. Our ability to behave properly carries us through the rest of our lives and helps us become successful citizens. Yet, teaching and guiding good behaviors can be one of the most frustrating aspects of parenting. Many times, parents "become very" frustrated because they find themselves in power struggles with their children. Another frustration is that children seem to take so long to learn good behaviors.

The Good Behavior Book is written to address one of the biggest frustrations and challenges of parenting. First, it helps parents to create an environment of consistency for their children. When inconsistencies are eliminated, children learn good behaviors much more quickly. Second, by very clearly demonstrating to the child that you are in complete control, power struggles happen less often.

The Good Behavior Book was not written to be a complete guide to parenting. Rather, it was designed as a collection of tools to be used in teaching behavior skills to children. These are skills they will take with them and use for the rest of their lives.

When used properly, the techniques described in The Good Behavior Book will help to stop fighting, arguing, whining and talking back.

Before the publishing of The Good Behavior Book, many of these techniques have been available to parents only through mental health professionals (Social Worker, Psychologist or Psychiatrist). Unfortunately, until now, that meant that most parents and children couldn't learn and use these techniques.

It should come as a relief for you to know that it's perfectly "normal" for children to constantly be testing their limits with adults and other kids. Children are more insecure when they have inconsistencies in their life, or they don't know what their limits are.

The Good Behavior Book contains tools for parents to help set limits and to reinforce positive, lasting behaviors. In turn, this will make life around your house much more pleasant for everyone. One last thing before you begin. It's okay to not be perfect in the beginning. Be prepared to make a few small mistakes and adjustments. Remember though, you will succeed.

Congratulations in advance.

The Behavior Board

The Behavior Board has been designed by child behavior specialists and parents, as a simple yet effective tool to mold children's behaviors.

If you have more than one child in the house, they should each also have their own Behavior Board and be playing the game. If they are not included, siblings will resent not being given a chance to play. Accordingly, if one child Is using the board and the other children aren't, he or she will resent having to earn rewards when the others don't the program will fail if all children, in the house, aren't playing the game.

Although these concepts seem simple, they have undergone extensive testing and trials on children of all ages. The Behavior Board will work as well for you as it does for professionals if these instructions are followed to the letter. You may be tempted to take what you think are shortcuts, but it is very important that you follow each step. The techniques must be followed exactly. To help you understand the use of The Behavior Board you should read straight through this chapter one time. This will help put the whole program in perspective for you. Following that, reread portions to the point that you are instructed to stop reading and begin writing, observing, or talking with your child (or children).

CHAPTER 1
Using the Behavior Board

Overview

The concept of the Behavior Board adults has been exposed to, at one time or another. By using Positive Reinforcement, the Behavior Board sets up a system of rewards for good behaviors. This system is called Token Economies. This means that the child earns points or stars (tokens) for certain behaviors and is able to spend these tokens to buy something that they desire.

Good vs. Bad Behaviors

If you want your child to exhibit "good" behavior, you have to first decide, very specifically, what behaviors you think are "good."

When you say, "Mike is a bad boy," you are speaking of specific instances; what did he do to make you think he is "bad"? To simply say he or she is "good" or "bad" leaves a great deal to the imagination and only reflects your opinion of a child's behavior at a specific time.

What you must learn to do is to separate the child from the behaviors. In other words, it isn't the child that is good or bad, it's their behaviors.

Another important point is that generalities have no place in a behavior management program. We must deal only with specifics-specifics such as "talking politely" or "eating all of their dinner."

In order to better understand your child's behaviors and your own expectations, you will need to spend some time observing, labeling (pinpointing) and tracking behaviors.

Observation

The observation period will take 3 or 4 days unless your child's behavior varies greatly. Seven days is a maximum observation period. Even though you know your child well, do not skip the observation period. Experience has shown that this observation period is mandatory.

Pinpointing (labeling)

During the observation period one of the things you will be doing is labeling your child's different behaviors. This labeling is called pinpointing because it very precisely identifies specific behaviors. These behaviors are either positive (good behavior) or negative (bad behaviors).

GOOD vs BAD

Example of Positive (Good) Behaviors	Examples of Negative (Bad) Behaviors
* Getting dressed by _ am	*Not sharing
* Turning out the light	*Whining
* Doing dishes (or helping with)	* Talking back
* Setting table	* Yelling indoors
* Brushing teeth	* Slamming doors
* Putting away toys	* Teasing
* Emptying trash	* Not minding (following directions)
* Making bed	* Wetting bed or self
* Taking bath	* Arguing
* Doing what is asked (minding)	* Being uncooperative
* Getting dressed	* Crying
* Going to sleep quietly	* Interrupting
* Washing car	* Fighting with brother, sister or friends
* Feeding pet	* Disobeying
* Finishing dinner in miutes	* Breaking _____ rules
* Cleaning their plate	
* Mowing lawn	
* Walking dog	
* Getting to school on time	
* Brushing hair	
* Sharing toys	

*Examples of suggested beginning behaviors see page 25 Establishing Priorities

Notice on the two lists on the previous page that the behaviors are very specific. Examples of behaviors that are not specific are "being nasty to parents" or "playing nicely." Remember, generalities have no place in a behavior management program because they only leave room for misinterpretation, arguing and inconsistency between parents and child.

Tracking

Tracking behaviors means counting each and every behavior you have pinpointed. Tracking is necessary to objectively establish frequency and patterns of certain behaviors. (This in itself can be quite an eye-opening experience).

Starting the Observation
Pinpointing and Tracking Period

To begin, you will need two sheets of paper for your lists. Label the top of one sheet "Positive Behaviors" and the other "Negative Behaviors."

Each time a behavior happens that you want to track, good or bad, write it on the appropriate list. Each time the behavior occurs again make a mark next to the behavior. If the behavior occurs for more than one minute, make another mark for each minute.

Both parents or authority figures, should participate in observing and collecting data, for example one during the day and one in the evening. If more than one person is observing the child, compare notes.

When patterns emerge, you will gain some insight into these behaviors. This recording process often results in a positive change in the child's behavior. As you are pinpointing, recording and tracking behaviors on your lists, the child may become curious about this activity. When they ask, calmly and briefly explain what you are doing and why.

After your first few days of pinpointing behaviors, call a special family meeting to explain why you are making the lists.

Mom: *"Debbie, your father and I have been making lists of your good behaviors and some behaviors we'd like to help you change."*

Debbie: *"Why?"*

Dad: *"Because in the next few days we will be starting a new game around the house to reward you for your good behaviors and to help you to stop the behaviors that your Mom and I don't like."*

Mom: *"Your Dad and I will be watching and keeping track of your behaviors on these lists, just like we have the last few days."*

Share your lists with the child; however, it is important that you don't argue or speak down to the child. Ignore any negative comments about the lists or your right to track their behaviors. You are the parent(s) and you do have the right to do this.

Mom: *"When we start the game, we'll write some of the behaviors that you need help with on this Board."* (Show them the Behavior Board)

Debbie: "*The Behavior Board?*"

Dad: "*That's the name of the new game.*"

Mom: "*Right, and we'll write the behaviors here. Then we can pick rewards together that you can earn and write them in here and here.*"

Debbie: "*Sounds like fun!*"

Dad: "*In a few days we'll talk more about how to play the game.*"

Debbie: "*OK*"

When an event occurs during the observation period, label it, write it on a list, and verbalize the negative behavior to the child.

As an example: *"You're not obeying"* or *"You're arguing"* or *"That's an interruption."*

Continue with your pinpointing and tracking for the remainder of the observation period.

Goal Setting

At the end of the entire observation period (3 to 7 days), set aside an hour or so for reviewing your results and goal setting.

Start with the most frequently occurring positive behaviors (those that occur more than once every two hours) and transfer them to another piece of paper. These behaviors are already occurring frequently enough that no improvement is needed. Chances are that you are already reinforcing these behaviors in your child.

Next take the least frequently occurring negative behaviors, those that you consider not to be serious problems at the moment. These are behaviors that don't need an intensive program to change right now.

From your two lists you now have goals that are: the most frequently occurring negative behaviors, and the least frequently occurring positive behaviors.

To finish setting goals, think about other goals not covered on your lists. When setting these goals, it is important to remember to set goals that aren't too far out of reach. In other words, you need to lay out small steps to reach your goals.

As an example of a goal: You'd like your child to be a better student. Decide what means specifically.

Does it mean you want them to get more A's, more B's, or more C's?

In this example, decide what small steps are necessary to get there.

Maybe this semester you can aim for more B's as a goal and use more A's as a goal for next semester. Some small steps toward that goal might be: If your child finds it difficult to study for more than 15 minutes at one time, your goal is studying for 20 minutes each day. If they are having more difficulty in one or two subjects, you goal would be to increase study in one subject by 5 additional minutes each day.

Begin by setting a timer in the room for 20 minutes. Do this for one week, then add five minutes per day each week. Each and every time the child can study until the timer goes off, praise them and award points or stars. By using these small steps, you will have helped the child develop good study habits within several months.

Another example of a goal is: You'd like your child to "be on time to school." Does that mean 8:00 or 8:15? Does that mean getting to the bus stop by 8:00 am? If so, you might have two goals, Goal Number 1 is "Getting out of bed and dressed by _____AM," and Goal Number 2 would be "Out the door or to the bus stop by_____ AM."

Another example of a goal is: Your child would like to learn to play the piano.

Does that mean one hour of practice per day? Or 30 minutes?

Although these are examples and your goals may be very different, they illustrate that it is mandatory that you take small steps toward your goals.

At this point you should have plenty of (ideas) to begin working with on your Behavior Board.

You should now have goals that are:

1) the most frequently occurring negative behaviors (these you want to weaken),

2) the least frequently occurring positive behaviors (these you want to strengthen), and

3) other goals that you feel are important.

Rewards and Reinforcers

Giving your child rewards (including points, stars or "tokens" and the rewards or privileges that they can buy with those tokens with those tokens) reinforces the behaviors they performed to get those rewards. Remember, rewards reinforce behaviors.

The kinds of rewards you choose will depend on your circumstances and the way your child responds to different rewards.

Social Rewards

Attention, affection, praise, favorite activities and knowledge of results are social rewards.

These kinds of rewards are often used by many families now and should be a part of your program also: "Debbie, thank you for turning off the light when you left the room."

They must be used whenever a child exhibits behavior that you are strengthening. It is these kinds of social rewards, working hand in hand with the Behavior Board, that will build lasting positive behaviors.

Tangible Rewards

Money, food, toys, special movies or programs, going to movies, an overnight with a friend and the like are concrete rewards. These rewards are best used with social rewards because by using tangible rewards with social rewards, you are creating a system that will continue to work as various aspects of the program are phased out. Phasing behaviors off the Board will be discussed in more detail at the end of this chapter.

Establishing Priorities

It is best that a major change in behavior not be used in the beginning. Remember to take small steps, especially at the start of the program.

It is very important that your child earns points every day. If parents don't make it easy enough to earn points, children lose their motivation and interest to play (or participate).

The "goal behaviors" you choose after trying out a few easier and less important behaviors, should be those that have the highest priorities to you. Initially they should also be goals that have the highest likelihood of succeeding. Some examples of behaviors that are good goals to start with, are marked with an on the positive and negative behavior lists (on page 5).

Starting the Game

There are only five write-in spaces so that too many behavior goals are not being worked on at one time. The program would be overwhelming for you and your child if you tried to change more than five behaviors at once.

Now it is time to involve your children. They will already have some idea of what you will be doing because you shared some things about the program with them several days ago. Begin by explaining the idea of the program to your child.

After the behaviors are written onto the Behavior Board, the program should be presented to the child as a game.

Dad: *"That's right, Debbie, we are all going to play a game that will help our family be happier."*

Mom: *"It will help Dad and I stop yelling at you and it will help you to do what Dad and I ask."*

Mom: *"Debbie, remember a few days ago we talked about your behaviors and the lists we were making?"*

Debbie: *"Yeah, you said you were going to give me rewards for doing some things, right?"*

Dad: *"That's right Debbie. We've listed some behaviors here that you have trouble with. Let's talk about them and how the game works."*

Mom: *"Your Dad and I have listed the behaviors that we want to give you rewards for doing. Now we're all going to play and work together so you can earn the most points and buy more rewards."*

Debbie: *"Tell me how it works"*

Dad: *"Every time you do any of these things (pointing to the chart), you'll earn a star (or point). You have to let us know when you think you have earned a star and we'll let you know when we think you have earned one."*

Mom: *"And then, at the end of every day, we will add up your stars, like this."*

Dad: *"Then you can use the stars you earned that day to buy rewards. And you keep saving your stars for weekly rewards, also."*

Debbie *"Rewards? What kinds of rewards?"*

Mom: "Well, we have a few examples of rewards you might want to earn every day and some other rewards you can earn weekly"

At this point show the child the list of rewards below and/or a list of your own. You should also decide how many points each reward costs, as well as other rewards the child would like to earn.

Daily Rewards

Snack (gum, candy. fruit, etc.)

Extra bedtime story TV per half-hour

Frozen yogurt or ice cream Phone call per 15 minutes Friend over for dinner

Over to a friend's for dinner

Stay up late per 15 minutes

Special dessert

Pick dessert for the whole family

Weekly Rewards

Friend overnight

Outing with mom and/or dad Movie

Rent video movie or cartoon Camping out

Small toy, book or coloring book

Go to library Favorite meal

Special toy

Picnic with family

Staying out late per half-hour

Dad :"*Debbie, what rewards would you like to add to the list?*"

Debbie: "*I'd like to add this, this and this" Pointing to the rewards list.*"

Mom: "*Good choices*"

Debbie: "*This sounds like a fun game, when can we start?*"

Dad :"*Mom and I thought we would get started today.*"

Debbie: "*Great!*"

Mom: "*O.K Now let's find a place to put the Board.*"

There is a space marked "Other Behaviors." This space is to be used in the event that your child does something special that should be rewarded-much like a "Bonus."

Using the "Other Behaviors" line gives you the ability to acknowledge special good behaviors and to keep them in perspective with the rest of the program. Using this space also gives you the ability to decide the point value of the behavior and when it will be used. As an example:

Dad: "*Debbie, it was very nice of you to help Mom in with the groceries. Let's give you an extra point for that.*"

When explaining the rules and object of the game to the child, make your instructions sound easy. Keep the program simple so that children always understand it. Also, keep the behaviors very specific so there are no misunderstandings. It is mandatory that daily and weekly rewards be used for children under 12 and older children that have a learning disability.

When your Behavior Board has been filled out completely by you and your child, it's time for the game (program) to begin. Put the Behavior Board up where everyone can see it. Some families put the Board on the refrigerator or dishwasher and some families put the Board on a wall.

Here is Debbie's Behavior Board all filled out at the beginning of the week.

The Behavior Board

Name: __Debbie__

Last Week Total: _____

Behaviors	Sat	Sun	Mon	Tues	Wed	Thurs
Making Bed						
Ready for school by 8am						
Finish Dinner						
Talking Politely						
Following Directions						
Other Behaviors						
Daily Totals						

Daily Rewards

1 extra bedtime story	5 pts
Snack Fruit	5 pts
Stay up 15 minutes late	8 pts
Ice Cream	8 pts
3 minutes of TV	8 pts

Weekly rewards

- Special movie at home
- Park
- Go to library
- Small toy
- Coloring book
- Kite Flying
- Favorite meal

And here's how Debbie did after her first week on the program.

The Behavior Board

Name: Debbie
Last Week Total: _____

Behaviors	Sat	Sun	Mon	Tues	Wed	Thurs
Making Bed		1	1		1	1
Ready for school by 8am			1	1	1	1
Finish Dinner	1	1			1	1
Talking Politely	11	111	1	11	111	11
Following Directions	11	1	11	1111	11	111
Other Behaviors						
Daily Totals	5	6	5	7	8	8

Daily Rewards

1 extra bedtime story	5 pts
Snack Fruit	5 pts
Stay up 15 minutes late	8 pts
Ice Cream	8 pts
3 minutes of TV	8 pts

Weekly rewards

- Special movie at home
- Park
- Go to library
- Small toy
- Coloring book
- Kite Flying
- Favorite meal

Giving Stars (or Points)

When you notice a behavior take place that's on the Board, you must give verbal reinforcement (social reward):

Dad: *"That was very good, talking politely to Mom, Debbie. Let's give you a star."*

Verbal reinforcement is very important when giving stars or points.

Mom: *"You put away your toys, that's great; let's give you a star."*

Verbal recognition gives reinforcement as important as the star, and your child will love the attention.

This reinforcement will also be important when phasing a behavior off the Board.

At the end of the first week first be sure to have your child spend the rewards or agree to transfer them to the next week. As you do this, point out the areas of progress, as well as behaviors that still need work. Then just transfer behaviors that will stay on the board, and any new behaviors to the new board, transfer appropriate star from the previous week and start over. Isn't that easy?

At this point you have plenty of information and you're ready to try the first week on the program. Before you start, here are a few reasons why the program has not worked well with some families.

Points are too hard to earn. Are the behaviors too difficult for the child? If so, make them easier.

This happens more commonly at the start of the program.

Rewards aren't what the child really wants. Talk this over with the child. If the rewards aren't what they want, think of new rewards together. It is very important to involve the child in the rewards they will be earning.

Rewards cost too much. Reduce the price of rewards. Have a sale!

Changing Behaviors and Rewards

Children can change rapidly. By the end of the second week you should have noticed some changes around the house.

Perhaps your child doesn't want to earn certain rewards? This is one of the simple and easy features of the program and the Board itself. It's easy. Remember, though, no changes to the Board unless everyone agrees.

By the end of the third or fourth week, if some behaviors are very consistent, you will need to phase out those behaviors from the list and add new ones. Here's how to do that; Talk with the child and explain that he or she has mastered, or become very good at, this behavior, and that you are taking it off the Board. It is important here to be sure the child knows they will still get praise from you for the behavior. They need to know that you have other behaviors that you want them to learn and start working on together to help keep life happy at home.

Dad: *"Well, Debbie, you've done really well at talking politely to Mom and me, and we want you to know how much more pleasant it's been around the house. We have another behavior that we want to start working on together that we're going to put in its place on the Board."*

Mom: *"We still want you to remember to keep talking politely to us and we'll thank you for that whenever you do it."*

If you encounter a lot of resistance here, you can wait another week to phase out some consistent behaviors. You must eventually replace bchaviors when they become very consistent. It is mandatory that daily and weekly rewards be used for children under 12 and older children that have a learning disability.

Answers to Frequently Asked Questions About the Behavior Board

Q: How long should I try the program before I give up?

A: For most children there is no point at which you should give up. To give up with a "normal" child is essentially throwing in the towel. Unless your child has a severe learning disability or other underlying medical or psychological problem, the program will work.

Q: What should I do if my child becomes bored or uninterested in the game (program)?

A: If your child is becoming bored or uninterested you need to look at several possible pitfalls including:

Are you using rewards that the child wants? If not decide with the child on new rewards. You should be able to find something that your child is willing and able to earn. Are the points too hard to earn? You should be sure that you are setting goals that are small steps. If you make the goals too far out of reach the child will never get there. This can be frustrating for everyone.

Do the rewards cost too many points? Talk this over with the child. Either reduce the price of the rewards or find smaller rewards that the child can earn more easily.

Does the child understand how to play the game?

Explain the game again in more simple terms. It is very important that the child understands how to play, or they won't participate.

Are you expecting changes too soon? You can't phase out behaviors too quickly.

Give the child the opportunity to earn some rewards with a consistent behavior before phasing it out. Is the child able to earn rewards daily?

This is very important in children under 7 or 8 years of age. Daily rewards must always be used with younger children. Even if you have an older child, daily rewards are an excellent motivator with all ages.

Q: What if my child displays an exceptionally good behavior not listed on the Board?

A: This is the time to use the line on the Board labeled "Other Behaviors." But remember, don't give away the farm. Always keep the whole program in perspective. In other words, don't make the point value of the "Other Behaviors" so high that the child can get the rewards they want by doing special things and ignoring the rest of the program.

Q: Should my child be allowed to write on the Board?

A: Yes. Children enjoy drawing their own stars or adding their own points to the Board. Children's involvement and interest in the game is very important. It is best, however, for parents to write in the behaviors and rewards so the Board looks neater. This also makes it easier for parents to be aware of the daily stars or points earned by their children. This will provide extra encouragement and discourage any potential "fudging" on points.

There is an occasional child that will try to add points that they didn't earn or erase behaviors. This should be dealt with as quickly as any other form of dishonesty. It may even be a behavior to work with on the Behavior Board. In the event that a problem of this type occurs, the Board should be placed out of the child's reach (but still visible to the child). They will then have to earn the right to write on the Board again.

Q: In a family of 2 or more children should I use the program with all of the children? or can I use it on one child and not the others?

A: If you have more than one child in the house, they should all have their own Boards, and all be playing the game.

Children will resent you not giving them a chance to play if they are not included.

At the same time, if they are using the Board and the other kids aren't, they will resent having to earn rewards when the others don't. The program will be likely to fail if all children aren't playing the game.

Q: My child is very stubborn and seems to always do just what he wants. Can the Behavior Board solve this behavior problem?

A: Yes, it can. In fact, the Behavior Board is a program that allows the child to earn rewards that they want. The child's motivation for doing what you want is to get what they want. If they aren't willing to earn their right to do what they want, don't give them privileges that they want.

Time Is On Your Side

Next we will focus on how time can be used constructively in your behavior management program.

As long as your child can count to ten, you will find the techniques in this chapter very useful.

A portable timer, such as those used in cooking, will be needed to put some of these techniques to work.

CHAPTER II

Counting

Counting to ten, as simple as it sounds, can be an excellent tool in a behavior management program.

This technique is used as a warning system. It is valuable in getting the child's attention and compliance before a privilege is removed or a punishment instituted. It also gives the child a "last chance" before being punished. Here's an example of how counting is used:

Mom: *"It's 8 o'clock, time to get ready for bed Jody. Go brush your teeth and get into your pajamas."*

Debbie: No reply.

Mom: *"Debbie, did you hear me?"*

Debbie: *"Yeah, I heard you; I'm watching TV right now."* (Or even if the child still doesn't respond and you're sure they heard you ...)

Mom: *"You know the TV is supposed to be off at 8 o'clock. Get up and start getting ready for bed."*

Debbie: No reply.

Mom: *"I'm going to count to 10! If you don't get up and start getting ready for bed by the time I reach 10, you will lose half your bedtime stories."*

You can use other appropriate privileges, depending on your child's age and values.

Examples include:

half your television or telephone time tomorrow and / or going to bed 30 minutes earlier tomorrow.

Still no reply (or "Wait a few minutes; I'm doing so and so" or whatever the excuse to stall for time).

Mom: *"One, Two, Three, Four, Five."* (as she gets up)

Debbie: *"All right, all right, I'm going."*

Mom: *"Okay, I'm up to Five. Any more delays and I'll start counting again."* Counting this time begins with the number six and continuing until you reach ten. Although this technique may seem a little harsh to some at first, it has proven to be a very effective tool when used properly.

Some important points to remember when you're using counting:

In younger children the most immediate form of consequences will be the most effective in behavior change. As an example, in the evening, if your child is still young enough that they have bedtime stories, use the withholding of half of the bedtime stories as the consequence for non-compliance.

In the morning or afternoon losing half of television or play time would be appropriate, again emphasizing the most immediate available consequence must be used in younger children.

When choosing a consequence use one half of a privilege or activity to be withheld rather than the entire privilege. There are two important reasons for this. They are: In most cases, it is too harsh of a penalty to lose a whole privilege (story time, television, telephone or play time). If the child continues noncompliance, you still have something in reserve to withhold, i.e., the other half of whatever you withhold. Meaningful consequences are the key to success because children, like adults, are motivated by different things at different times. Therefore, you need to change consequences to fit the circumstances, the child's mood and situation.

Some examples of this point include;

If a child knows that you're having strawberry shortcake for dessert, and they don't like strawberries, "withholding dessert" as a consequence isn't likely to work well, or If you decide to use "withholding half of their telephone time," when their best friend is out of town, it will have very little meaning to them and will not serve as a consequence or motivator.

By the same token using "one half of television time" as a consequence, on a night that nothing is on T.V. that they want to watch, won't work either.

In other words, you need to be aware of what consequences are meaningful to the child at the time. Don't be willing to fall back on the same old consequences if you expect this technique to continue working (don't overuse the same consequences).

Even if dessert is something they like, if you withhold dessert frequently, children may tend to minimize the importance of dessert. It somewhat disables the use of this technique if you become lazy in its use.

Always be prepared to back up your statements about consequences. If you tell the child that they will lose either one half or all of something, and they continue in their noncompliance, do what you said you would do.

Count at a reasonable speed. Don't count so fast that the child has no time to respond, or so slowly that they doubt your sincerity. An appropriate rate is one number every second.

Counting can easily be used with older children as well: **Dad:** ***"Mike, I asked you 15 minutes ago to take out the trash."*** (wash the car, mow the lawn, etc.).

Mike: "I heard you; I'm still on the phone."

Dad: "*Mike, I'm going to count to 10. If I get to 10 and you're not on your way to take the trash out, you'll lose 30 minutes of television time today.*" (or you'll have to be home 30 minutes earlier tonight, Friday night or whenever you choose).

Mike: "*Yeah, sure, Dad I'll be off the phone in a few minutes.*"

Dad: "*You said that five minutes ago! One, Two, Three, Four, Five, Six ...*"

Mike: "*I'll call you right back, Sharon. I'm on my way, Dad.*"

Dad: '*Thank you, Mike.*"

With all ages it is extremely important that you: Follow through: If you tell the child you will withhold something, and they haven't complied by the time you get to 10, inform them of the lost privilege. Don't forget to use social rewards when the child complies. Say "Thank you for... "

Give clear instructions about what is expected, when it is expected, the time(s) it is expected and show them, if necessary. To be sure they understand, ask them to repeat the instructions or to show you. Give the child time to comply before using counting.

Mom: "*Mike, I asked you to empty the dishwasher 10 minutes ago.*"

Mike: "*Can't I do it later?*"

Mom: "*No, I'm sorry, Mike, I need you to do it now so I can put dirty dishes inside.*"

Mike: "*Oh, come on, Mom!*"

Mom: "*I'm going to start counting.*"

Mike: "*You don't have to, I'm coming.*"

Mom: '*Thank you, honey.*"

After you begin to use counting, the child becomes used to how it works as well as the consequences. Often then it is only necessary to tell them that you are going to start counting, before they comply.

When using this technique over the long term the child begins to understand the importance of the tasks you want them to perform. When used with the Behavior Board, they will learn that these tasks will need to be done before counting becomes necessary if they expect to receive points or stars. Most of the behaviors on the Board should be set up so that points (or stars) are not given if counting becomes necessary.

Mom: *"Deb, it's time to wash your hands for dinner."*

Debbie: (yelling) *"I don't want to!"*

Mom: *"That's an outside voice, Debbie. You don't want to what?"*

Debbie: (whining) *"I don't want to eat dinner now."*

Mom: *"It looks like you're not going to earn any points today on your Behavior Board, for not whining."*

Debbie: (still whining) *"I don't want to eat dinner now" (getting louder) "and I want my points!"*

Mom: *"Debbie, you aren't going to get anything by whining. Stop whining now or I'll start counting."*

Debbie: (still whining) *"I don't want to eat dinner. All I want is to keep playing."*

Mom: *"If you're still whining when I get to 10 you're going to Time Out."* (Time out is explained just ahead.)

Debbie: (whining louder) *"I want to keep playing."*

Mom: *"One, Two, Three, Four . . "*

Debbie: (whining) *"I don't want to have dinner."*

Mom: *"Five, Six, Seven, Eight, Nine, Ten. You're still whining, honey. Come on."* (Taking Debbie by the hand) *"You're going to Time Out."*

Debbie: (screaming, crying) *"I don't want to go to Time Out."*

Mom: (still walking towards the Time Out area) **"I told you, honey, if you didn't stop whining you would have to go to Time Out."**

Debbie: (crying) **"I don't want to go to Time Out! I won't like you if you put me in there."**

Mom: "You'll be in Time Out for five minutes." (setting the timer) **"Your time starts when you're quiet."**

CHAPTER III

Time Out

What Exactly Is Time Out? Let's first talk briefly about what Time Out isn't.

Time Out is not angrily yelling at the child. It is not "Get into your room until I say you can come out." Time Out is not taking a child from a bad situation and sending them somewhere else where they can do what they want while the adults don't have to think about them.

There are some parents who say, "Oh, I've used that technique before, but it didn't work." Taking a closer look at what they did use reveals:

The child was not sent to Time Out (or their room) every time it was appropriate. The room used was usually their bedrooms that were full of toys, books, TV, radio and most anything else the child needed to make the situation bearable, if not downright enjoyable. When the child was sent to Time Out (their room), it was for much too long, usually 30 minutes or more.

Now, let's discuss what Time Out is:

Time Out means time out or away from (positive) reinforcement. The child is removed from the situation reinforcing or causing the problem. They are placed in a Time

Out area where there are no reinforcers. This means nothing that would be a distraction for the child; no toys, books, people, TV, or anything else positive.

The place you pick for your Time Out area should be dull and non-reinforcing. It should have a door to isolate it from the rest of the family and house. It should not be dark or frightening for the child.

The most likely spot in the home, and the one used by most parents, is a bathroom. If your child is very aggressive or destructive, it may be necessary to remove breakable objects.

When to Use Time Out?

You have already learned how to handle many kinds of behavior using techniques described earlier.

Therefore, Time Out should be used either alone or to complement other behavior management techniques dealing with disruptive behaviors.

These include:

- **Temper tantrums**
- **Fighting**
- **Teasing**
- **Yelling indoors (after being told to stop)**
- **Name calling**

- **Other high rate (frequency) negative behaviors**

*High rate (or frequency) negative behaviors are those that repeat themselves many times over a short period of time.

Time Out should also be used for another group of behaviors called disruptive noncompliance. These are behaviors like willful disobedience, defiance and when counting has not worked well. (An example of this is when you've taken away as much as you can that day-all of a bedtime story, TV or telephone time.)

How to Use Time Out

There are several important things to do before you use Time Out for the first time.

First, you'll need to have your timer handy. Second, you will need to be ready with a system of reinforcers and consequences to be used with Time Out this means that when the child goes to Time Out and follows all the rules, you'll need to give them praise and/or thank them. It also means that if the child doesn't follow the Time Out rules, you must inform them of and enforce the consequences. So, you'll need to determine the consequences before starting to use Time Out. (We'll give you some examples later.)

Third, explain to the child all about Time Out and when you'll be using it. Remember to include how long the child will be in Time Out.

Fourth, practice using Time Out with the child before you use it the first time. Show them the Time Out area and timer. This is so that you don't find yourself trying to explain Time Out to an already upset child.

Fifth, you will need to go over these rules for Time Out with the child:

• When told to go to Time Out, stop whatever you are doing and go directly to the Time Out area.

• No arguing or debating about using Time Out.

• Time Out starts when you're quiet-no yelling, crying or making noise.

• Once in Time Out, stay there until the timer goes off. Leaving Time Out before the timer goes off starts the time over again.

And Sixth, after Time Out is over (not before), reinforce with the child that you care about them and that you are trying to help them with certain disruptive behaviors.

Parents should also observe the following rules about Time Out:

• **Always remain calm when using Time Out.** When using Time Out, calmly take the child by the hand to the Time Out area, close the door and start Time Out.

• Always use short periods of time. Research from the 1960's has shown that short periods of Time Out are just as effective as longer periods. The best rule of thumb to use is one minute of Time Out for each year of age. For a 5-year-old use 5 minutes of Time Out, 6 minutes for 6-year-olds, and so on. This is in addition to penalty time added on for breaking Time Out rules.

• **Be consistent.** If you have decided to use Time Out for certain behaviors, always use it for those behaviors. Inconsistencies will seriously undermine your efforts to weaken problem behaviors. No lecturing or arguing about Time Out, calmly explain why they are going to Time Out one time only. Each time the child tries to argue the point add one extra minute of time.

• If the child breaks any of the Time Out rules, enforce the consequences.

• If the child was sent to Time Out for non- compliance, repeat the request that they didn't comply with, after they are out of Time Out. If they still do not comply, send them back to Time Out Do this as many times as necessary to ensure compliance.

• If the child does any damage in Time Out, they must be held accountable for the damage. Although this happens infrequently, some children will try damaging or breaking things while in Time Out in an effort to get your attention or "pay you back" for sending them there. Because of the willful nature of this behavior the child must be made to fix, help fix or pay for (in a material way) the damage. Examples of this include handing Mom or Dad tools to fix the damage or mopping up the water on the floor.

• Remember to reward for following Time Out rules by using praise and/or a "Thank you."

Although we discussed this in Chapter 1, it's worth repeating that the child must be able to receive positive reinforcement and rewards routinely so that they aren't displaying negative behaviors to get attention from you.

Mom: *"Debbie, Dad and I are going to start something new around the house called Time Out."*

Debbie: *"What for?"*

Dad: *"You and Mom go inside for a minute. That's great, now we'll shut the door so you can see what the timer sounds like from in there."* RING

Dad: *"Mom and I want to help you stop fighting and help to keep you from having your tantrums."*

Debbie: *"What's Time Out?"*

Mom: *"See, that was easy to hear, wasn't it?"*

Debbie: *"Well, yeah, I guess so. I don't like Time Out! I don't want to do it!"*

Mom: *"Time Out is a place that we'll have you go when you start fighting or have one of your tantrums."*

Dad: *"Honey, we really care about you and the way you act. That's why we're going to use Time Out. If Mom or I send you to Time Out, you have to go. "*

Debbie: *"How does it work?"*

Mom: *"Whenever your dad or I tell you to go to Time Out, we'll have you go upstairs to the bathroom. Next, we'll set*

Time Out

the timer for 5 minutes." (Debbie is five years old.) ***"Then we'll shut the door and you have to stay in here until the timer goes off."***

Mom: *"That's right, Deb, we're just explaining before we use it, so you'll know what to expect, not to see if you'll like it. Do you understand, honey?"*

Debbie: *"Yeah, I guess so."*

Time Out Away from Home

When you are using Time Out at home it's important that it be used when you are away from home as well. Although it is more difficult and inconvenient to use away from home, Time Out, with a few modifications, can and should be used in most settings that you are likely to find yourself in with your children.

In the Car

If the child's behavior gets out of hand when you are traveling in the car, this simple procedure can be used.

Without becoming distracted from your driving responsibilities, try using counting to end the disturbance (in the case of fighting or some other disturbance).

"I'm going to count to three, if you don't stop you will be in Time Out when we arrive at_ _ _ _".

If the disturbance continues add 5 minutes to the Time Out. If the disturbance still continues, or if counting is not appropriate, slow down and pull off the road. If you're on a busy highway, it's best to get off at the next off ramp. Only after pulling off the road do you inform the child that you are going to put them in Time Out. This will avoid the danger of being distracted by a child, arguing or yelling about having to be in Time Out.

Once off the road, stop the car and inform the child about why you are putting them in Time Out. Just as at home, don't argue or discuss it with the child. At this point everyone, except the child needing Time Out, must get out of the car. Inform the child that the Time Out area is the car and everyone else is getting out until Time Out is over.

Other than these details, using Time Out in the car has the same rules as using it at home.

In a Restaurant

To use of Time Out in restaurants a safe area outside must be available, and an adult must stay with the child. Alternatively, some adults favor taking the child to their car for Time Out at restaurants.

In Retail Stores

While using Time Out in retail stores is more inconvenient for the adult, it can and should still be used in this setting.

Dressing rooms in clothing stores make an excellent place for the Time Out area. If this proves impractical, simply take the child outside for Time Out.

If you have to use Time Out often while shopping with children, it might be worthwhile to leave the child at home or in someone else's care while you're shopping.

In Grocery Stores

Leaving a grocery store for Time Out can prove to be impractical. If it is not, take the child outside the store, and/or to the car, for Time Out.

If it is impossible or impractical to use Time Out then and there, you must inform the child that they are to go to Time Out as soon as you get home. When you arrive back home, it is important that you follow through with Time Out.

CHAPTER IV
Other Uses of Time

Setting Time Limits

Many people, adults included, have trouble judging how much time has passed. This is true when you're doing something you are enjoying or when something you dislike has your attention. We've all heard the expression "Time flies when you're having fun."

Children seem to have more difficulty with the passing of time than adults do, for two excellent reasons.

First, because they are relatively inexperienced (compared to adults) in judging when a measure of time has passed, and second, up until approximately the age of seven, most children cannot tell time well. If you cannot tell time, 10 minutes or one-hour passing is very abstract. You may have noticed that up until age five or six or older with some children, something that happened last week may still be referred to as yesterday.

Likewise, when you tell a child that they can do an activity for 10 minutes or they must stop an activity in 10 minutes (or a half hour or whatever), they are almost always upset when you tell them that "Time is up."

Addressing all of these problems is very simple. Setting time limits will teach children about the passage of time periods. It is also much easier on parent and child.

All that is needed in setting time limits is your portable timer and some brief instructions to the child.

To begin, set your timer for whatever length of time you want to allow before an activity is to stop or start. Like everything else, it also requires some advance instruction and explanation to the child.

Dad: *"Debbie, remember how Mom and I used this timer"* (showing Debbie the timer) *"for cooking and for Time Out?"*

Debbie: *"Yeah, what about it?"*

Dad: *"Mom and I have noticed that you need a little help in figuring out how much time has gone by when you're doing something you really like."*

Mom: *"From now on, until you can tell time better or learn to judge time better, we're going to use this timer to help you remember how much time has passed."*

Debbie: *"How are you going to do that."*

Dad: *"As an example Deb, if Mom or I want you to only watch TV for a half of an hour, we'll set the timer for 30 minutes, like this" (setting the timer) "and when it rings, like this" (Ding) "we'll all know it's time to turn the TV off."*

Here are some other examples of using a timer to set a limit on an activity:

- Telephone time
- Bath or shower time
- Getting ready for bed
- Getting dressed
- Getting ready for school
- Playtime
- Use of the bathroom
- Homework
- Television time
- Game time

Here's an example of using time:

Mom: *"Debbie, I'm setting the timer for 10 minutes. When it rings, I want you to turn the TV off, no matter where you are in the program."*

Debbie: *"Why, Mom?"*

Mom: *"Because we're going to eat dinner soon and I need you to help me set the table."*

Debbie *"How about 20 minutes, Mom?"*

Mom: *"I'm setting the timer for 10 minutes. Remember, if you turn the TV off and set the table when the timer rings, you'll earn points on your Behavior Board."*

When the timer went off, Debbie set the table, just as her mom had asked.

Mom: *"Thank you for helping me out and setting the table. Let's give you a point on your Behavior Board."*

In this example the Mom explained what she expected to be done and when. Mom also set the timer for 10 minutes and left the timer out where Debbie could see it clearly. When Debbie finished setting the table Mom thanked her (social reward) and gave her a point or star on her Behavior Board (tangible reward).

The following are examples of using Time Out for different behaviors:

Teasing and Name Calling

Debbie: *"Michael is a dummy, Michael is a dummy, Michael is a dummy."*

Mom: *"I heard that, Debbie. You're teasing your brother. Let's go, I'm taking you to Time Out."*

Debbie: *"No. I don't think I should have to go. I was just kidding"*

Mom: (taking Debbie by the hand) *"Here we are in the Time Out area. You'll be here for 7 minutes."*

Since Debbie is 7 years old Mom sets the timer for 7 minutes and closes the door.

Debbie: *"Michael is a dummy, Michael is a dummy. "*

Mom: *"I'm resetting the timer. Time Out starts when you're quiet"*

"I heard that! go to Time Out!"

Debbie: "*Oh, all right, I'll be quiet.*"

When the timer goes off, Debbie opens the door and starts playing quietly.

Mom: "*Thank you, Debbie, for finishing Time Out quietly I only had to remind you once.*"

In the above example, Mom quickly interrupted Debbie for teasing, and calmly took her to Time Out.

During Time out, she reminded Debbie about the rule for being quiet. After Time Out, Mom gave Debbie a social reward for completing the rest of Time Out quietly.

Several pages ago we gave an example of a child who whined, cried and had a mild tantrum when sent to Time Out. This would be a good time to review that example.

Willful Disobedience

Dad: "*Mike, I asked you to clean up your room earlier. Why didn't you do as I asked?*"

Mike: "*No reply (he's watching TV).*"

Dad: "*I gave you a chance; now I want you to clean your room and, I'm sorry, but you won't earn any points for doing it!*"

Mike: "*Then you can forget about it! I'm not cleaning my room today!*"

Dad: "*You're disobeying me. I want you to go to time out now for 10 minutes.*" (Mike is 10 years old)

Mike: "*No way!*"

Dad: "*Okay, that's one more minute for not minding.*"

Mike: "*You must be joking. Why should I clean my room when I'm not going to get anything for it?*"

Dad: "*Keep arguing and not only will I add another minute to time out, but you'll go to bed 30 minutes earlier.*"

Mike: "*All right, all right, I'm going.*"

Dad: "*Thank you.*"

Mike goes to Time Out for 11 minutes and goes back to watching TV when he comes out.

Dad: "*Just because you went to Time Out doesn't mean you're excused from cleaning your room*"

Mike: "*Hey, that's not fair!*"

Dad: "*There's nothing unfair about it-you know the rules. If you're not on your way up to clean your room by the time I count to 10, you're going back to Time Out. One, Two, Three, Four, Five, Six, Seven, Eight, Nine, Ten.*"

Mike is still watching TV

Dad: "*Mike, go back to Time Out.*"

Mike: "*Come on, Dad!*"

Dad: "*Get back to the Time Out area now.*"

Mike: "*Okay, I'm going. For how long?*"

Dad: "*Ten minutes.*"

This time when Time Out was over, Mike cleaned his room.

Dad: "*Mike, thanks for cleaning your room.*"

Mike: "*Hurmp*"

You just read an example of a child testing limits with his Father. The father started by informing Mike of the consequences of not cleaning his room. He then informed Mike that he was disobeying him and of the consequences of that, which was Time Out. Mike disobeyed again and his Dad added on time to Time Out.

When Mike came out of Time Out the first time, he thought his dad wouldn't push the subject anymore. However, once you decide to make rules, you must enforce them.

In this case, Mike's Dad had to send Mike back to Time Out a second time before Mike cleaned his room. He also had to be prepared with another consequence (going to bed 30 minutes early) if Mike still refused.

You also saw an example of using counting to let the child know that you're serious. In most cases the child would have gone to clean his room just about the time Dad started to count, if not before then.

Yelling Indoors

In this example Debbie has "talking quietly indoors for one hour" on her Behavior Board chart, because she uses her outside voice often indoors.

Debbie: (yelling to her mom, who is 15 feet away) *"Hey, Mom, can I watch TV?"*

Mom: *"Well, Debbie, here's one more hour you won't learn a point for talking quietly indoors. Yes, you can watch TV"*

Debbie: *(10 minutes later, yelling) "Can I have a cold drink?"* (Mom is still 15 feet away.)

Mom: *"Debbie, that's the second time this hour that you yelled indoors. Turn the TV off I'm taking you to Time Out for 5 minutes."* (Debbie is 5 years old.)

Debbie: *"Come on, Mom, I won't do it again."*

Mom: *"Let's go."*

Debbie: *"I don't want to!"* (yelling)

Mom: *"That's one more minute for yelling."* (shutting the door to the Time Out room)

Mom: *"Time Out starts when you're quiet."*

In this example you saw Time Out being used with the Behavior Board for yelling indoors, a disruptive behavior. Since the child had already yelled indoors once that hour, and missed an opportunity to earn a point, another behavior weakening technique (Time Out) is used when the behavior is repeated that hour.

Fighting and Noncompliance

Debbie: *"Ow! That hurts, Mike."*

Mom: *"What's going on?"*

Mike: *"Debbie is using my notebook paper."*

Debbie: *"Didn't know it was his. He didn't have to hit me!"*

Mom: *"Michael, I want you to apologize to your sister and then go to Time Out for 11 minutes."* (Mike is 11 years old.)

Mike: *"Forget it!"*

Mom: *"That's one more minute in Time Out for disobeying. Go to Time Out now. I'll set the timer for 12 minutes."*
Mike goes to Time Out and when the timer rings;

Mom: *"Michael, your time is up. I want you to apologize to your sister for hitting her."*

Mike: *"No way!"*

Mom: *"Okay, Michael, back to Time Out for 11 minutes."*

Mike: *"Fine."*
The timer rings and Mike comes out of Time Out.

Mom: *"Michael, apologize to your sister."*

Mike: *"Okay, okay. Debbie, I'm sorry for hitting you."*

Mike was originally sent to Time Out for hitting his sister. By not complying with his mom's request to apologize to his sister, one minute was added to the Time Out.

When he came out of Time Out Mike was again told to apologize to his sister. He refused again and was sent back to Time Out. Had he refused when he came out the next time he would have been sent back again. Instead, as most frequently happens, Mike apologized to his sister.

We sincerely hope that the techniques that we have described have helped you and your family. If these techniques have not made a measurable change in behavior, our advice is to seek help from a mental health professional such as Social Worker, Psychologist, Psychiatrist or Family Counselor.

Make photocopies before using the last Behavior Board chart.

Name: _____

Last Week Total: _____

Behaviors	Sat	Sun	Mon	Tues	Wed	Thurs
Daily Totals						

Daily Rewards | **Weekly rewards**

THE Behavior BOARD

Name: _____

Last Week Total: _____

Behaviors	Sat	Sun	Mon	Tues	Wed	Thurs
Daily Totals						

Daily Rewards | **Weekly rewards**

Name: _____

Last Week Total: _____

Behaviors	Sat	Sun	Mon	Tues	Wed	Thurs
Daily Totals						

Daily Rewards   **Weekly rewards**

Name: _____

Last Week Total: _____

Behaviors	Sat	Sun	Mon	Tues	Wed	Thurs
Daily Totals						

Daily Rewards   **Weekly rewards**

Name: _____

Last Week Total: _____

Behaviors	Sat	Sun	Mon	Tues	Wed	Thurs
Daily Totals						

Daily Rewards   **Weekly rewards**

Name: _____

Last Week Total: _____

Behaviors	Sat	Sun	Mon	Tues	Wed	Thurs
Daily Totals						

Daily Rewards **Weekly rewards**

Name: _____

Last Week Total: _____

Behaviors	Sat	Sun	Mon	Tues	Wed	Thurs
Daily Totals						

Daily Rewards   **Weekly rewards**

Name: _____

Last Week Total: _____

Behaviors	Sat	Sun	Mon	Tues	Wed	Thurs
Daily Totals						

Daily Rewards | **Weekly rewards**

Name: _____

Last Week Total: _____

Behaviors	Sat	Sun	Mon	Tues	Wed	Thurs
Daily Totals						

Daily Rewards **Weekly rewards**

The Behavior Board

Name: _____

Last Week Total: _____

Behaviors	Sat	Sun	Mon	Tues	Wed	Thurs
Daily Totals						

Daily Rewards | **Weekly rewards**

www.ingramcontent.com/pod-product-compliance
Lightning Source LLC
Chambersburg PA
CBHW080925170426
43201CB00016B/2264